BRITISH LUXURY CARS
OF THE 1950s AND '60s

James Taylor

SHIRE PUBLICATIONS
Bloomsbury Publishing Plc

Kemp House, Chawley Park, Oxford OX2 9PH, UK
1385 Broadway, 5th Flr, New York, NY 10018, USA
29 Earlsfort Terrace, Dublin 2, Ireland
Email: shire@bloomsbury.com

SHIRE is a trademark of Osprey Publishing, a division
of Bloomsbury Publishing Plc

First published in Great Britain in 2016 by
Shire Publications

A CIP catalogue record for this book is available from
the British Library.

James Taylor has asserted his right under the
Copyright, Designs and Patents Act, 1988, to be
identified as the author of this book.

Shire Library no. 832

Print ISBN: 978 1 78442 064 2
ePDF ISBN: 978 178442 187 8
ePub ISBN: 978 1 78442 186 1

Designed by Tony Truscott
Typeset in Garamond Pro and Gill Sans.
Printed in India by Replika Press Private Ltd.

21 22 23 24 25   10 9 8 7 6 5 4 3

The Woodland Trust
Shire Publications supports the Woodland Trust, the
UK's leading woodland conservation charity.

www.shirebooks.co.uk
To find out more about our authors and books visit
our website. Here you will find extracts, author
interviews, details of forthcoming events and the
option to sign-up for our newsletter.

COVER IMAGE
A 1964 3.8 litre Jaguar Mk 2.

TITLE PAGE IMAGE
Many of the British luxury car makers went to the wall
before the 1960s were out. This is the sphinx bonnet
mascot of one of them, Armstrong-Siddeley.

CONTENTS PAGE IMAGE
The Humber's dashboard blended transatlantic styling
ideas with the traditional British reliance on wood.

ACKNOWLEDGEMENTS
Alamy, cover image; Charles01/Wikimedia, page 49;
James Taylor, pages 1, 8, 9, 12, 30, 36, 37, 40, 41
(both), 42, 43, 48, 59 (bottom), 60, 62 (bottom);
Kent Police Museum, pages 14, 38 (bottom); Magic
Car Pics, pages 3, 4, 6, 7 (bottom), 10, 13, 17, 21
(both), 23, 24, 26, 27, 28 (all three), 29, 32, 33
(both), 34, 38 (top), 44, 46, 47, 50, 51 (both), 52,
53 (both), 54, 56 (both), 57, 58 (both), 59 (top), 62
(top); RREC, pages 7 (top), 15, 16, 19, 20 (both), 22.

CONTENTS

WOLSELEY

...a luxurious way of motoring

INTRODUCTION

In the 1950s and 1960s, class distinctions were still very much part of the British national consciousness. Although the Second World War had gone a long way towards breaking down what remained of the old class structure after the Great War of 1914–1918, notions of 'them' and 'us' still shaped many aspects of British social behaviour. One of the aspects they affected was that of car ownership.

To some extent, it was a question of price: cost put most luxury cars beyond the reach of the average family. But, as is the case today, older luxury cars became more affordable when second-hand, and their buyers were able to enjoy their perceived superiority over more ordinary cars as well as benefit from their more luxurious specification. So demand for these cars remained strong after their first owners had moved on to something newer.

Right at the top of the car hierarchy were the twin marques of Rolls-Royce and Bentley. Traditionally, Rolls-Royce made 'The Best Car in the World', and few buyers knew or cared that this description was a trademark rather than an independent assessment. Rolls-Royce had asserted this position before the Great War and there was still no reason to believe otherwise. It was not until the early 1960s that Mercedes-Benz in particular made a determined attack on the Rolls-Royce market.

So, as the car maker at the top of the hierarchy – although the small volumes it made meant it was far from the largest

Opposite: The cachet of leather upholstery was used to help sell a derivative of the big Austin, in this case badged as a Wolseley. The elegant female hand with its expensive jewellery is all part of the image.

Vanden Plas had been a traditional coachbuilder before the Second World War. BMC bought it out in 1946 and used its name and expertise on luxury cars and limousines like this one. The basic design remained in production under different names for twenty years.

The Autocar, November 26, 1948

THE

Vanden Plas

PRINCESS

COACHBUILT SALOON
on the Austin 135 Chassis

A Car for To-morrow . . .

A modern expression of the coachbuilder's traditional art happily complementing the reliability of the automobile engineer's latest achievement

VANDEN PLAS (ENGLAND) 1923, LIMITED. KINGSBURY WORKS, KINGSBURY, LONDON, N.W.9. *Telephone* : COLINDALE 6171-2.

– Rolls-Royce set the standard for others to follow. Despite changes made in the late 1940s to cope with a harsh economic climate, a Rolls-Royce was still a very superior kind of car, and its characteristics influenced the designs of other less expensive luxury saloons.

Britons at the start of the 1950s expected a luxury saloon to meet certain criteria: it needed to be large and impressive, and obviously superior to even the most expensive family saloons. It had to have a turn of performance that would

Luxury cars were an important attribute of every VIP. Here, a chauffeur-driven Rolls-Royce Silver Cloud collects Hollywood actress Joan Crawford in Johannesburg in 1957.

At a time when vinyl upholstery was becoming increasingly popular, leather took on its own cachet of exclusivity. This advertisement features the Daimler One-O-Four luxury saloon.

leave ordinary family cars behind, although neither sporty handling nor exceptional speed were requirements. It needed spacious passenger accommodation with room for a division to be fitted behind the front seats so that rear-seat occupants could enjoy privacy while a chauffeur drove. A large luggage boot was also important.

Upholstery had to be made of leather or, usually in limousines, the West of England woollen cloth that was less affected by extremes of temperature. When vinyl upholstery became more common in 1950s cars, it was deemed by many to be just that – common – and was not under any circumstances to be found on the seats of a luxury model. Top-end models often had leather or cloth on the door trim panels, although vinyl here was acceptable. Wood trim was an essential. At the very top of the market, carefully matched figured veneers and even inlaid wood finishes were expected, although by the end of the decade, there was acceptance for simpler and plainer wood finishes.

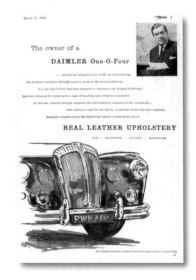

The owner of a

DAIMLER One-O-Four

REAL LEATHER UPHOLSTERY

Luxury cars needed large and powerful engines to propel their bulk and weight at respectable speeds, and by the middle of the 1950s, it was widely accepted that anything smaller than 3 litres was insufficient because such engines generally lacked the necessary power and accelerative ability. The term '3-litre class' came to define the luxury class, and both Rover (in 1958) and the British Motor Corporation (for their Vanden Plas model in 1959) chose the '3-litre' name for their cars. It did not only define engine size; it also made clear that these cars were intended for customers of high social rank. The class distinction between these types of cars and more ordinary models was undisputed at the time, as was the distinction between the ordinary middle class and upper middle class, which it more or less paralleled.

Luxury car engines had to be as smooth and refined as possible. The four-cylinder engine of the typical family car

The smoothness of a large-capacity, multi-cylinder engine was an important luxury car ingredient. This is the 3-litre six-cylinder in a Humber Super Snipe of the early 1960s.

was too rough in operation for a luxury model, and so the typical luxury car engine of the 1950s and 1960s had six cylinders. It was not until the dawn of the 1960s that Rolls-Royce moved to a V8 engine, partly to pander to US market tastes, and only after that did Daimler and Rover introduce V8 engines to the luxury saloon market.

Inspired mainly by American examples, some British luxury car makers developed V8 engines. This was the highly regarded 4.6-litre V8 in Daimler's 1961 Majestic Major saloon.

All these characteristics created a very distinctive kind of car that was not made in any other country in the world. It was so steeped in the traditions and expectations of the British class system that its appeal was limited outside the UK. Anglophiles and expatriates bought them, but as symbols of wealth or achievement, these cars were something of a puzzle to non-Britons. While the Rolls-Royce name was universally known as a symbol of excellence, and the Jaguar name as a symbol of performance, other makers often struggled to find buyers outside the UK for their luxury saloons.

Close behind Rolls-Royce and Bentley in prestige came Daimler, which had provided cars for the royal household

Lagonda built sporting carriages for gentlemen, and their 3-litre model came as a saloon with two or four doors, and as a drophead coupé. This advertisement captures the image that the cars had in the 1950s.

throughout the 1930s and still produced craftsman-built machines of exceptionally high quality. However, Daimler had also decided to appeal to a wider customer base, and, even though it disguised this bid for sales by using its subsidiary Lanchester marque, this ensured it could never again have the same status as Rolls-Royce.

If Rolls-Royce, Bentley and the top-model Daimlers were for the landed gentry and the wealthy upper middle classes, there were still some highly respected marques on the next rung down the social ladder: Armstrong-Siddeley had a long history, and made some luxury saloons of very high quality during the 1950s; Alvis had become popular during the 1930s as a sporting rival for Bentley, and its cars were seen as fitting for gentlemen; and Lagonda was in much the same position.

These makers traded on exclusivity. Their cars were expensive, and as they were only affordable by the wealthy they became symbols of wealth. That the pool of potential customers was relatively small had never been a deterrent in the 1930s, although in the changed social and economic conditions of the 1950s it did become a problem. The only solution was to increase sales by lowering the entry-level price of ownership, and that inevitably led to at least the perception that standards were also being lowered.

An even bigger problem was that when a maker like Armstrong-Siddeley or Daimler tried to move into a different sector of the market, it found the volume-car makers already well established there. The smaller upper-crust companies could not compete on price, and their names and images were not enough to attract sufficient customers. One by one, they went to the wall. Lagonda folded in 1957 (though it was revived unsuccessfully in the early 1960s), and Armstrong-Siddeley was wound up in 1960. Daimler was forced to sell out to Jaguar in 1961, and Alvis to Rover in 1965, although both marques remained available in name.

In the meantime, the big-volume car makers had seen their opportunity and exploited it ruthlessly. Humber had been the luxury marque of the Rootes empire since the early 1930s, and was respected as a maker of affordable luxury saloons. From the mid-1950s, its luxury saloons shared much of their basic engineering and appearance with cheaper middle-class models, so saving on manufacturing costs and enabling the company to keep prices down. The formula proved very successful. In the changing times of the 1950s, even the wealthy did not always wish to be tarred with the brush of snobbery. So a car that appeared unostentatious but was much better equipped than lesser models found a ready market: it allowed the wealthy to have their cake and eat it at the same time.

Snobbery also affected Jaguar's reputation. The company's sporting saloons were deliberately designed to appeal to would-be Bentley owners, and although their build quality was not in the same league they had a powerful appeal. This deliberate attempt to emulate Bentley prompted old-school criticism of Jaguar cars as lacking what Britons saw as 'breeding'. However, strong sales enabled Jaguar to keep prices down, and high performance fostered a public perception that the cars were exceptional value for money. Little by little, Jaguar secured a place among the luxury car makers, achieving sales volumes that were the envy of some established mass-market manufacturers.

There was no such problem for Rover, which had for many years enjoyed a solid reputation as a maker of cars for the British professional classes – doctors, lawyers and bankers. Though a small independent company, it sold far more cars than the old-established luxury car makers and, by comparison, qualified as a volume manufacturer. Rover brought an element of middle-class common sense to the party with its 3-litre saloon in 1958, which initially targeted Humber and Armstrong-Siddeley customers, and the make's reputation was such that buyers readily accepted the newcomer. Over the next decade or so, this sober and affordable but well-finished saloon would become the major player in the British luxury saloon market.

Very much the runner-up in the status game was BMC, which owned the Austin and Wolseley marques. Both were mass-market names, and over the years both had fielded large and formal saloons for buyers who wanted a grand car but could not afford the high prices of the traditional luxury car makers. Yet the mass-market names had an image problem, and when BMC decided to break into the growing market

Though fashions had changed by the late 1960s, the British love of wood and leather had not. This was the interior of the Rover 3.5-litre saloon, which boasted a V8 engine plus standard automatic gearbox and power-assisted steering.

for 3-litre luxury models in the late 1950s, it revitalised an old brand to help it do so.

In fact, the Vanden Plas name had been around for many years on BMC limousines that sold as hire cars and as mayoral transport. Austin had bought the remains of the old-established coachbuilder in 1946, and had used its name on top models ever since. By the late 1950s, BMC was trying to save costs by making variations of a single design serve the expectations of customers for more than one marque, and introduced no fewer than three variants of the same car. Different trims and the different associations of the marque names helped create Austin, Wolseley and Vanden Plas versions.

Though essentially the same car, they catered very well for a growing market. The Vanden Plas model and its successor were effective and cheaper rivals for the Rovers and Humbers of their time. Only further mergers within the industry, which from 1968 saw the BMC marques, Jaguar and Rover all subsumed into British Leyland, led to the demise of Vanden Plas, although its name survived as an indicator of high equipment levels on other cars.

By the end of the 1960s, the traditional British luxury car was effectively obsolete, although Rolls-Royce and Bentley survived as an international force and would maintain the characteristics of the type for many more years. The real problem was cost. The business model followed by Humber

A refined car could only become more refined, obviously, and that was the theme of this advertisement for the Mk II version of the Vanden Plas Princess 3-litre. Underneath the sophisticated exterior, the car was really a big Austin.

The powerful engines and capacious bodies of some luxury models also made them favourites with Britain's police forces. Kent Police bought this Austin A110 Westminster in 1966.

and BMC made best sense, and other makers created new luxury models by loading lesser cars with extra equipment. To keep these cars competitive on price, that equipment was never as lavish as in the traditional British luxury car, and the Ford Granada or Vauxhall Senator of the 1970s were simply not in the same mould as what had gone before. Meanwhile, global expectations of the luxury car were changing under the impact of new designs from companies such as Mercedes-Benz.

The final nail in the coffin came when the oil crisis of 1973 pushed fuel prices up to uncomfortably high levels. On the second-hand market, nobody wanted an old luxury car that struggled to better 15 mpg and demanded careful and regular upkeep. Many became cheap caravan tugs and were scrapped when repair costs became high; others were simply neglected and finished their lives as banger racers. Although Rolls-Royce and Bentley models had a status which denied them this fate, it was only a rare few examples of most other British luxury models that survived to be treasured by enthusiasts, and which serve as a reminder of how things were in the heyday of the type.

THE PINNACLE: ROLLS-ROYCE AND BENTLEY

LONG BEFORE THE 1950s dawned, Rolls-Royce and Bentley had staked their claim to the top positions among luxury cars in Britain – and in most countries around the world. By this stage, they were united marques, as Rolls-Royce had bought the bankrupt Bentley concern in 1931, and during the 1930s had exploited the marque's sporting heritage to widen its customer base. In the straitened economic circumstances of the 1940s and early 1950s, however, the two marques would grow even closer, one becoming more or less a clone of the other.

Rolls-Royce and Bentley cars were much more expensive than those of any other British manufacturer. In 1955, for example, the entry-level Bentley saloon cost £3,295 before tax and the Rolls-Royce equivalent cost £3,385. These were the

The Rolls-Royce and Bentley models were aimed at the British upper classes, and at anybody else with the money to afford them. This left-hand-drive car was delivered to Scottish actor James Robertson Justice during his time in Canada.

The Standard Steel saloon appeared first as a Bentley Mk VI, and only later as the Rolls-Royce Silver Dawn, seen here in left-hand-drive export form. The styling was both conservative and elegant, and very much of its time.

Standard Steel cars (with all-steel bodywork volume-produced to standardised designs), which were built in relatively small numbers on a production line. For the more exotic coach-built models, prices simply went up and up. It was not hard to spend well over £5,000 before the addition of purchase tax when most other luxury cars of the time cost around £1,200 before tax. The average family saloon was more like £500, and a small saloon much less.

So ownership of a Rolls-Royce or a Bentley made a strong statement of wealth about its owner. Prestige went with that. Britain's class system, though gradually breaking down by this stage, also affected the way that the general public saw them. These were the cars of the landed gentry and the former aristocracy, and of those who had done well in business. They were, then, the cars of the bosses – the mill-owners, factory owners, and so on.

The owners themselves were more likely to see buying one of these cars as an expression of their good taste and good breeding, those qualities associated with the top end of the British class system. They expected the cars to reflect that, in ways that lesser and cheaper models simply could not.

Rolls-Royce knew exactly how to keep their customers happy. Although the advent of the Standard Steel saloons after the Second World War had introduced a new era of standardisation, there was no loss of quality. Rolls-Royce was able to draw on the expertise of its subsidiary Park Ward, one of the independent coachbuilders who had produced bespoke bodywork in earlier times. So the leather used for Rolls-Royce (and Bentley) upholstery was not just leather but the finest Connolly leather. The wood was not just polished timber but handcrafted sections of figured wood with carefully matched veneers. The carpets were not a gesture towards the comfort of the drawing-room at home but were top-quality Wilton, typically with wool over-rugs.

All this was expensive, and so was the engineering that went into the company's cars. Actual performance was not a particular concern; far more important were smoothness and silence of operation, plus of course absolute reliability. The large-capacity engines did give good performance, but more significant was that their size allowed them to be

The Bentley Mk VI set the style for the luxury cars of the late 1940s and early 1950s, with an all-wooden dashboard, central instruments, wooden door cappings and a big steering wheel. The upholstery was leather, of course.

under-stressed, thereby minimising mechanical commotion and wear. Today, a drive or a ride in one of these grand cars remains an awe-inspiring experience, conveying a sense of luxury and well-being that few other cars of the time could even approach. There was, and remains, something indelibly patrician about the Rolls-Royce and Bentley models of these two decades: they were imbued with the traditional values of the English gentleman.

The post-war era had brought a radically new approach for Rolls-Royce and Bentley. Until this point, they had built only the chassis, which would then be supplied to a coachbuilder for bespoke bodywork. After 1945, however, it was clear that this was going to become the exception rather than the rule. So Rolls-Royce developed a single chassis design (which could be lengthened if necessary) and a single six-cylinder engine (which could be offered in different states of tune) and, with these, a Standard Steel body that would be built for them by specialists Pressed Steel at Cowley, in Oxford. The emphasis on 'steel' in its name reflected the dramatic change from earlier times. This body was pressed and stamped from steel, just like those on less expensive cars. It was no longer coach-built by hand on a wooden frame, although the body shells would be trimmed and finished by hand in the traditional way to preserve the Rolls-Royce quality.

The change was so radical that Rolls-Royce chose to proceed cautiously. So the first of the new Standard Steel cars carried the Bentley name, to protect the primary brand in case there was an adverse public reaction. The Bentley Mk VI could be bought as a chassis-only for delivery to a coachbuilder of choice, but by far the majority carried the Standard Steel body. This had a restrained, dignified design that reflected contemporary taste for razor-edge styling but remained carefully aloof from it. It was sold as a 'sports saloon', as befitted the Bentley name. Not until 1949 was the same car, albeit with detuned engine, released as a Rolls-

Royce Silver Dawn, and even then it was available only for export until 1953.

So the 1950s opened with the Rolls-Royce Silver Dawn and Bentley Mk VI saloons in production. Changes arrived in 1951, when the engine was enlarged to 4.5 litres to give 100-mph performance (at least in the Bentley) and in 1952, when a larger boot made the Bentley an R-type, although the Rolls-Royce remained a Silver Dawn. An automatic gearbox also became available in 1952 to meet demand, although Rolls-Royce had to do things their own way. They bought in the Hydramatic gearbox from General Motors in America, but they used a British-built fluid flywheel between engine and gearbox instead of the American torque converter.

The engine was meanwhile enlarged to 4.9 litres for the last of the high-performance Bentley Continentals based on the R-type, and this also went into the new model introduced in 1955. This time, Standard Steel Rolls-Royce Silver Cloud and Bentley S-type saloons were identical apart from radiator grilles and other identification – not that it mattered, because the new body style, created in-house at Rolls-Royce, was an absolute masterpiece. It succeeded in being elegant, dignified,

Common mechanical elements were at the core of the Rolls-Royce policy after 1945. This Silver Wraith is a formal limousine, but shared much of its running-gear with the standard saloon models.

Stunningly beautiful in every detail, the Silver Cloud set the standard for the later 1950s and early 1960s. They were available with Bentley badges too, when they were known as S-types.

A subtly sloping bonnet and fashionable twin headlights characterised the Silver Cloud III models from 1963. Elegance was still the keynote, although performance had been increased with a new 6.2-litre V8 engine.

conventional and yet contemporary all at the same time, while offering more space than before, thanks to a longer-wheelbase chassis. A few chassis were custom-bodied, but most customers were very happy with the Standard Steel offering. At this stage, the slightly cheaper Bentley considerably outsold the Rolls-Royce version, and some commentators have argued that cost was not the key factor, but rather a form of inverted snobbery that reflected a reaction against the old British class system.

This basic design remained available for ten years, undergoing several improvements on the way. Power-assisted steering and air conditioning became options from 1956, and

Even though this dashboard is in a 1963 Silver Cloud, it has barely changed from the 1955 original. Instruments are grouped in the centre again. The matching veneers, leather upholstery and woollen carpets are of the highest quality.

there was even a long-wheelbase limousine option from 1957. Sales in the USA were vital, and from 1959, the Silver Cloud II and Bentley S2 had a 6.2-litre V8 engine that matched US expectations of a V8 in top models. From 1963, the Silver Cloud III and Bentley S3 took on fashionable (and practical) paired headlamps, together with a more raked bonnet-line to modernise their appearance.

These cars, of course, all had a separate chassis, not least because that allowed maximum design flexibility. Elsewhere, though, separate-chassis construction was disappearing in favour of monocoque construction, where the body is built as a self-supporting 'box'. Rolls-Royce knew they would have to go that way eventually, and the car that replaced the Clouds and S-types in 1965 was indeed a monocoque.

It was sold as the Rolls-Royce Silver Shadow and the Bentley T-type, and the two were absolutely

The Silver Cloud was still the benchmark luxury car in the early 1960s. Note the armrests, the ample legroom and the general ambience of luxury in this 1963 Silver Cloud III.

The Silver Shadow had the job of taking Rolls-Royce into the second half of the 1960s and on into the 1970s. Though perhaps a less attractive design, it still had what was considered the right degree of British understatement and dignity about it.

identical apart from grilles and other identification. Their shape was squarer, in the 1960s idiom, but as always they acknowledged contemporary taste without submitting to it slavishly. Though undeniably less attractive than the cars they replaced, the Shadow and S-type were again dignified and very slightly aloof in appearance, with beautifully balanced lines.

On the inside, they cosseted occupants with the usual impeccable blend of wood and leather, and came with the modern comforts of air conditioning (fitted in the majority of these cars) and electric windows (provided as standard). On the mechanical side, there were now all-round disc brakes with vacuum servo assistance (Rolls-Royce had always favoured a mechanical servo before then), plus a complex and sophisticated self-levelling suspension system that was operated by high-pressure hydraulics. An automatic gearbox

Though different in detail, the interior of the Silver Shadow encapsulated the same qualities as that of its predecessor. There were high-quality materials, comfort and space, even if such things as electric windows had now modernised the picture.

was the only option: Rolls-Royce and Bentley owners did not have to change gears for themselves, any more than they had done when they had employed a chauffeur to do the driving.

'This big, luxurious car accelerates very quickly up to 90 mph, giving absolutely no sign that it is hurrying' wrote John Bolster in *Autosport* during 1967. He described its cornering power as 'phenomenally high for such a big car'. Its 'great complexity and elaboration of design makes driving easier and safer than ever before. It is a wonderfully untiring car for long journeys … but above all … it is *fun* to drive … I am at a loss to understand how it can be made for its admittedly high price. No car offers greater value for money.'

These, then, were the standards that makers of less expensive luxury cars strove to emulate. A fundamental aim was stress-free motoring, created by the combination of a powerful engine with an automatic gearbox and, ideally, a soft-riding suspension. Increasingly, power-assisted steering became a necessity. The passenger cabin had to be trimmed in leather with polished wooden trim elements. And, from the outside, the car had to convey a sense of dignity and make clear to all the social status of its owner.

THE DAIMLER 3-LITRE 'REGENCY' SALOON

THE NEW DAIMLER CONVERTIBLE COUPÉ *on special series 3-litre Chassis.*

THE NEW HOOPER 'EMPRESS MARK II' SALOON *on special series 3-litre Daimler Chassis.*

THE DAIMLER 'STRAIGHT-EIGHT' HOOPER LIMOUSINE

see Daimler at the Motor Show

Don't miss the Daimler or Hooper stands, whatever you do! On them
you will find the complete range of magnificent cars built to a tradition
that makes a Daimler one of the most envied possessions in the world.

DAIMLER STAND NO.	**165**
HOOPER STAND NO.	**106**

THE   DAIMLER   COMPANY   LIMITED   ·   COVENTRY

THE OLD-ESTABLISHED NAMES: DAIMLER AND ARMSTRONG-SIDDELEY

B Y THE START of the 1950s, Daimler was one of the most prestigious names among British cars, second only to Rolls-Royce and Bentley. It was Daimler which had built the royal cars since the 1930s, Daimler which had put its name on countless armoured cars and scout cars for the army during the Second World War, and Daimler which created cars for the aristocracy and wealthy middle classes. Although there were volume-produced owner-driver saloons, the Daimler name suggested chauffeurs and bespoke coachwork. Indeed, to protect that image, Daimler's owners at BSA had absorbed Lanchester in 1932, using the name to create a range of cars for the merely well-off middle classes around Daimler engineering.

Typical of the bespoke Daimlers were the two large models introduced immediately after the war, in 1946. These were the DE27 and DE36, both built in penny numbers, and mostly as limousines with coach-built bodywork. Several entered service with the royal family.

No company could survive on such cars, and Daimler had an owner-driver range as well. A revived pre-war design served in the late 1940s, but the real post-war owner-driver Daimler arrived in 1951 in the elegant shape of the Regency. Sales were slow in its first three years, perhaps because the older Consort was still finding eager buyers. However, the chassis design and the new 3-litre (later 3.5-litre) six-cylinder engine would form the basis of many later Daimler models in the 1950s. It had

Opposite: This 1952 Daimler advertisement shows what the marque stood for at the time. At the top is the Regency saloon, with a DB18 drophead coupé below it and a DK400 limousine below that. At the bottom is one of the big formal limousines, a DE27.

This advertisement for the One-O-Four cleverly punned on the phrase 'the perfect company car'. It was not, of course, a company car in the accepted sense – but the idea of perfect company suggested sophisticated friends and high society.

Daimler's traditional preselector gearbox, which allowed the driver to select the gear in advance and engage it by pressing a floor pedal. Smooth changes were the result.

The Regency was mildly modified and given a more powerful engine option in 1954, and then transformed into the One-O-Four a year later, with yet more powerful versions of the same engines and the option of a Lady's Model.

This reflected the influence of Lady Norah Docker, wife of Daimler's chairman and instigator of some notable Daimler show 'specials' in the early 1950s, and included such extras as a built-in vanity case and a picnic case. Unfortunately, the Lady's Model did not sell and, as the standard One-O-Four was not doing well either, Daimler was forced to lower its prices in 1956. It was the start of a slippery slope.

The Regency also became the basis of the DK 400 or Regina model from 1955. Available with a coach-built Hooper body or a much less expensive in-house style, this replaced the old DE27 model as Daimler's prestige limousine. Although it survived until 1960, it was a very small-volume model which probably did little to help Daimler's balance sheet.

Meanwhile, there were less expensive Daimlers further down the range in the shape of the Conquest from 1953 and the Conquest Century (with 100 bhp) from 1954. Sales were healthier here, but these cars were up against formidable and cheaper competition from the middle-class Rovers, and it was hard to justify their higher prices. The Conquest disappeared in 1956 and the Conquest Century in 1958 – and by then, Daimler was in trouble.

The next few years were bridged by one of the company's most attractive models. The Majestic was a restyled derivative of the Regency/One-O-Four cars with a 135-bhp 3.8-litre

The distinctive shape pioneered at the start of the 1950s continued into the early 1960s with the Majestic Major, powered by Daimler's own 4.5-litre V8 engine and capable of an astonishing 120 mph. The two-tone paintwork was typical.

Figured wood, instruments in the centre of the dashboard and a huge steering wheel – this was the traditional British design for the Majestic Major.

The Majestic Major was true to type, with sumptuously comfortable leather upholstery, figured wood trim around the windows, and pull-down picnic tables for the rear-seat passengers. Above the rearmost side windows were dowager straps, designed to help elderly ladies make a dignified exit from the car.

version of the six-cylinder engine, power-assisted disc brakes all round and a proprietary automatic gearbox. Introduced in 1958, it carried on until 1962, by which time Daimler had been owned by Jaguar for nearly two years. As Jaguar had its own, far more powerful 3.8-litre six-cylinder engine, the Majestic was an inevitable casualty.

However, all was not lost. From 1960, Daimler had introduced a companion model – the Majestic Major – with a brand-new 4.6-litre V8 engine. Again with automatic transmission as standard, this was a superb car with a 120-mph top speed – far higher than most users of such a formal machine were ever likely to need. 'Dignified, but by no means stately or ponderous' was the *Autocar* verdict in 1961. 'It appeals almost as a sports saloon to the owner driver with

a large family … it is dignified and distinctive in a traditional way, yet the price is within the means of a great many people who favour a large car.' Those people would have to be wealthy, though: the car cost nearly £3,000, including purchase tax.

The Majestic Major was accompanied after 1961 by a long-wheelbase DR450 limousine version, capable of carrying up to six passengers in its rear compartment behind the standard division at speeds of up to 100 mph. Though expensive and rare, the latter was a bargain in its sector of the market and lasted, along with the Majestic Major, until Jaguar replaced the pair of them with the DS420 limousine in 1968.

There was no real replacement in the Daimler range for the old Conquest Century until 1966. Jaguar, eyeing Rover's inexorable move upmarket and into territory they considered their own, announced a Daimler-badged version of their own new 420 saloon. Sold as a Daimler Sovereign, it was both more luxuriously appointed and more prestigious than the Jaguar equivalent – and, inevitably, more expensive. It staked Daimler's claim in an important area of the market that the marque would exploit after 1969 with the new Sovereign, this time based on the Jaguar XJ6.

From 1968, Daimler switched to a new design, with a body built by Vanden Plas on the platform and running-gear of the big Jaguar 420G saloon.

For most of the 1950s and 1960s, Daimler's problem had been that it had too many small-volume models available. This product range was probably conditioned by its long history as a maker of bespoke cars, but it did not allow for the economies of scale achievable in volume manufacture. Daimler simply sold too few cars before its products became upmarket Jaguars, and lost its independence as a result.

Like Daimler, Armstrong-Siddeley was one of the old and respected names in the motor industry. It was associated with the Armstrong Whitworth aircraft company, and the link with aviation contributed to its image of high quality. Yet, despite some advanced engineering, Armstrong-Siddeley cars were mostly staid, and in the 1930s their customers had been the wealthy upper middle classes. They bought the cars because of their distinguished pedigree.

Armstrong-Siddeley re-entered the market after the Second World War with a series of models named after wartime aircraft and built on a common chassis. The Lancaster saloon, Typhoon coupé and Hurricane drophead coupé all continued

The Armstrong-Siddeley Whitley saloon was really a 1940s design, although it remained available until 1954. With a 2.3-litre engine, it was on the outer fringe of the luxury class.

into the early 1950s, and from 1950 were supplemented by the Whitley saloon and the 18-hp limousine on a lengthened wheelbase. Yet none of these had an engine larger than 2.3 litres, which was by this stage really too small for the luxury class. All had the option of being ordered with a Wilson preselector gearbox, which was made by a company within the same group and brought its own upmarket aura with it.

However, Armstrong-Siddeley had greater ambitions. By 1952, the company was ready with a new chassis and a new overhead-valve six-cylinder engine with a 3.4-litre capacity. With this came an impressive and stylish new body, elegant and spacious enough to suit the carriage trade while also subtly suggesting high performance. It even had a swept wing line and rear-wheel spats like the contemporary Jaguar Mk VII – and indeed was intended as a Jaguar rival. From 1955, there was a long-wheelbase limousine version as well, and the car came with a choice of Wilson preselector, manual gearbox (made by Humber) or, again from 1955, a US-designed automatic gearbox, as used by Rolls-Royce.

Following the aviation theme, the new car was known as the Sapphire, a name used on jet engines from Armstrong-Siddeley. *Autocar* thought it had 'a definite air of quality together with a very lively performance' when it was new in 1953, and was 'very good value for money in its class.' Unfortunately, it was not as fast as the Jaguar (91 mph versus 101 mph), and even though it undercut that model on price (just under £1,574 in 1953 compared with around £1,700), all that heritage counted for little. Armstrong-Siddeley sold just over 1360 examples a year on average before replacing the car in 1958, while Jaguar was turning out well over five times as many of its big saloons.

Jaguar's smaller saloons also outclassed two new Armstrong-Siddeley models that had been intended to secure a foothold in the solid middle-class market then largely dominated by Rover. The four-cylinder Sapphire 234 and six-cylinder 236

This is the new and luxurious car . . .
the Armstrong Siddeley

SAPPHIRE

Beautifully appointed . . . fast for the purposeful driver: docile in the town.
On the continental run . . . comfort and power to spare.
Four-speed electrically-operated Preselector gearbox: or alternatively four-speed synchromesh . . . as you wish. Over 120 brake-horsepower giving economical and fast motoring. Steering, brakes and road-holding are all superb.

Truly a Car of Character

£1110
Plus Pur. Tax £618 3s. 4d. Total £1728 3s. 4d.

See it at Earls Court. STAND 144.

THE NEW *Sapphire*

ARMSTRONG ⓐ SIDDELEY

Armstrong-Siddeley moved up a gear with the 1952 Sapphire. Even its appearance hinted at the big Jaguar Mk VII saloons with which it competed for sales. The 346 name came from 3.4 litres and six cylinders – precisely the engine specification of the Jaguar.

were introduced at the same time as the new Jaguar in 1955, and, despite some interesting technical features, were ugly and frumpy by comparison. They sold very poorly, and cost the company dear. By mid-1958, production was brought to a halt.

Undaunted, Armstrong-Siddeley revitalised the Sapphire from 1958 with a more powerful 4-litre engine, standard automatic gearbox and subtle but quite substantial styling changes. Power steering and servo-assisted brakes with discs at the front were now standard, and the car came with a unique rear-compartment heating system that also demisted the back window. In 1959, *The Motor* was most impressed by the new model, called the Star Sapphire; it was 'truly untiring to drive or to be driven in', and the review described the 'effortless high performance rather than sporting verve' of this 'high-quality car'.

However, the Star Sapphire was still no Jaguar. With a top speed of 104 mph when the latest Mk IX Jaguar was

The Sapphire's dashboard set the main dials ahead of the driver, and was another traditionally British all-wood design.

managing 113 mph, it cost nearly £2,500 in 1959, while the Jaguar was less than £2,100 with automatic gearbox. It was clear that the Armstrong-Siddeley marque was no longer competitive, and the company did not survive beyond the 1960 merger of its aero-engine business with the Bristol Aeroplane Company.

Figured wood and leather upholstery are complemented by no fewer than three armrests for the rear-seat passengers.

THE VOLUME PRODUCERS: HUMBER AND ROVER

H UMBER WAS AN important player in the British luxury car market of the 1950s and 1960s. In 1928 it was bought out by the Rootes Group, and from 1932, Humber became the combine's luxury brand. Humbers were large, dignified and luxurious, often with traditional wood-framed bodies that were constructed by Rootes' coach-building subsidiary, Thrupp & Maberly. During the Second World War, many senior British military officers used Humbers as staff cars, the most famous being 'Old Faithful', which belonged to Field Marshal Montgomery. Nevertheless, there were owner-driver models too, and these often shared some elements with the less grand Rootes marques such as Hillman.

As the 1950s opened, then, Humber was a highly respected marque, with a distinctly conservative image and a reputation for building cars that appealed to the carriage-trade – wedding and funeral businesses, official limousines, and the like. They entered the 1950s with three large models on sale, all powered by the same 100-bhp 4-litre six-cylinder engine.

The Super Snipe was the owner-driver saloon, built from steel but designed to look like the longer-wheelbase Pullman and Imperial limousines that were coach-built by Thrupp & Maberly. The coach-built cars lingered on until 1954, up-engined for 1953 to 4.1 litres, but the Super Snipe was completely redesigned in 1952, taking on the more modern looks of Humber's entry-level Hawk along with

Opposite:
The rear passengers in a Super Snipe enjoyed vast legroom, as well as the expected wood and leather.

Though designed as an owner-driver saloon, the Super Snipe of the early 1950s was a big car that would not have looked wrong with a chauffeur at the wheel. It was styled with a family resemblance to the larger Imperial limousine, which was coachbuilt.

that strong 4.1-litre engine and the option of an automatic gearbox. Nevertheless, it was still somewhat old-school in its engineering and disappeared in 1957. By that stage, Humber sales had begun to slide.

Rootes took a gamble in 1955 that an estate car would sell at this level of the market, and based theirs on the Super Snipe. It sold well enough to persuade the company to build an estate derivative of the replacement range as well. The Super Snipe estate had a virtually captive audience, with no direct competitors. It combined luxury and spaciousness – and in their declining years these cars were much liked by antique dealers. Rover did look at building a competitor in 1960, and BMC built a handful of estates from their Vanden Plas 3-litre in the early 1960s, including at least one that went to the royal family. But nobody seriously challenged the Humbers.

Humber prepared itself for the 1960s with a new all-steel monocoque that was used in both the Hawk (1957) and the new Super Snipe (1958). Styling suggested American influence, and these cars had a more modern six-cylinder engine of just 2.6 litres with similarities to the larger-capacity type used by Armstrong-Siddeley; there had indeed been some cooperation between the two companies. A more powerful 3-litre derivative arrived in 1959, along with front disc brakes, and a year later came a new front end with fashionable twinned headlamps, possibly the first on any British-built car.

The set was then completed in 1964, when the Super Snipe was restyled with a longer and more angular roofline, and was joined by a more expensive version called the Imperial. Both had the 3-litre engine, the better-appointed Imperial having power-assisted steering, automatic gearbox and a black leathercloth roof covering as standard.

These 1960s Humbers were still luxury cars in the old tradition, with elegant interiors featuring leather upholstery and beautifully finished polished wood trim which extended even to drop-down picnic tables. Thrupp & Maberly were responsible for trimming the top-end models. Once the

After 1957, Humber moved to a much more modern shape, inspired by American designs. This was the 1961-model Super Snipe, now with paired headlamps and even whitewall tyres to set off its two-tone paintwork.

If the Humber looked American on the outside, it could hardly have been more British inside, with figured wood, leather and even pull-down picnic tables.

Perhaps it was American influence that persuaded Humber to make an estate car derivative of the Super Snipe. No other British maker built one at this level of the market. This 1963 example became an accident response car with Kent Police.

3-litre engine had arrived, the cars were also capable of nearly 100 mph, and could accelerate with respectable speed and grace. Hard cornering was not in their nature, but few owners can have complained. 'Utterly restful to drive and equally applauded by the passengers [the Super Snipe] represents a very well worthwhile successor to a long line of illustrious cars that have carried the Humber name' was *The Motor*'s verdict in 1960.

Limousine derivatives proved quite popular too, and Super Snipes and Imperials were often to be seen ferrying senior government officials or on embassy duties in London. The load capacity of the Super Snipe estates (there were no Imperial equivalents) endeared them to several police forces because these big vehicles could carry the necessary equipment for dealing with the aftermath of accidents.

Rootes kept the showroom prices of its big Humbers comparatively low through economies of scale: they shared many components with other models and marques. So, despite their greater prestige, they were actually competing on price with models like the Vanden Plas 3-litre. At the 1960 Earls Court Motor Show, for example, the Vanden Plas with automatic gearbox cost £1,467 7s 6d, including purchase tax, while a Super Snipe with manual gearbox cost £1,488 12s 6d. By comparison with their real opposition, such as Rovers and Jaguars, these Humbers were excellent value for money.

Throughout the lifetime of these cars, Rootes saw no reason to lower showroom prices until the very end, when the 1967 models were discounted to clear stocks before production ceased that summer; on the contrary, Humber prices were gradually increased – and when purchase tax was reduced, as in 1958 and 1962, Rootes raised the ex-factory price of the cars while still allowing the customer some benefit from the smaller amount of taxation.

Rover, meanwhile, entered the luxury saloon market almost by accident. After the war, it had confined itself to solid and conservative saloons for the professional classes. The car which became its very successful entry to the luxury market had originally been intended as a smaller saloon, to sell in high volume and in direct competition with the larger Fords, but growing demand for the company's Land Rovers meant that there was no factory space to build it. So this second saloon range was re-envisaged as a larger, low-volume model.

Rover prepared the market for its new venture in the mid-1950s by introducing new and more expensive variants of its existing P4 saloon range, and in 1958 announced its new P5 model with the simple title of the 3-litre. At £1,763 17s 0d with a manual gearbox or £1,921 7s 0d in automatic form, the new P5 model was more expensive than the Humbers, just below Jaguar and at roughly the same level as Armstrong-Siddeley before their prices increased again. Nevertheless, it was the cheaper Humber that Rover always saw as their main rival, because it offered so much at its lower price. When

The Rover 3-litre provided strong competition for the big Humbers after 1958, when this example was pictured. Its simple, elegant design was much liked, and worked well with two-tone paint schemes.

Super Snipes did well in the 1961 East African Safari Rally, Rover followed suit with a team of 3-litres in the 1962 event.

The Rover benefited from an elegant blend of modern styling with old-school dignity, although early cars had some drawbacks. Despite its 3-litre capacity, the car could not reach 100 mph; its all-round drum brakes were distinctly marginal; and the absence of power-assisted steering made low-speed parking a chore. Nevertheless, it offered good room for six people, a large boot and a choice between bright two-tone modernity and conservative gravitas when finished in dark monotones. The interior combined modern design with traditional wood and leather, although on the first cars it was a little gaudy for some tastes.

The Rover was soon improved with a lower ride-height that gave better handling, a more positive gearchange and an overdrive as standard on manual-gearbox models, disc front brakes and the option of power-assisted steering. A power increase from 1962 made it a genuine 100-mph car, and toned-down interiors offered all the elegance that customers for this class of car wanted. High build quality and mechanical smoothness were further factors that made these big Rovers a success.

The dashboard design of the Rover was clean and modern, with plastic elements almost as prominent as the wood. This original design was considered rather fussy and was later simplified.

As the 1960s wore on, it was the Rover that rose to the top of the class. Despite its higher price, it outsold the Humbers, Jaguars, Wolseleys and Vanden Plas models that were its contemporaries, and after 1960 probably attracted many former Armstrong-Siddeley customers. Prices crept ever upwards. From 1962, the saloon model was joined by a four-door coupé, with a more streamlined roof profile and slightly more equipment at a much higher price. Without additional power, it never matched the performance of the more expensive Jaguars, but it certainly ate into their market by providing a rakish-looking and handier-sized alternative to the rather bloated Mk X saloons from the Coventry-based company.

Rover boasted royal connections for its 3-litre model too. Already a supplier of Land Rovers to the royal family for many

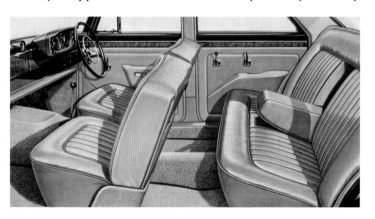

With thick leather seats and polished wood trim, the Rover delivered all the key elements of a traditional British design in a more modern form. This interior dates from the early 1960s, but the wood trim was never quite as heavily figured as the artist has suggested in this sales catalogue drawing.

The later Rovers had 3.5-litre V8 engines, inset foglights and chromed, styled wheels. This publicity picture conveyed the idea of gracious living.

years, in 1960 it delivered the first of several 3-litres to the Queen and the Queen Mother. Over the years, there would always be at least one P5 (and later, P5B) model on the royal fleet, and the Queen is said to have liked hers above all other cars for the occasions when she drove herself.

Prices continued to rise, the biggest jump coming in 1965 when the Mk III models were introduced, distinguished mainly by a more luxurious interior. These were the curtain-raiser for the P5B models announced two years later, which

came with a 3.5-litre light-alloy V8 engine that had been bought from General Motors in the USA for production in Britain. Both saloon and coupé variants now came only with automatic gearboxes, and both were much quicker than the old 3-litre models. 'Many who regard this Rover – with its wood-panelled interior and four thick, leather armchairs – as being the finest London club on wheels, will now have to accept it as being the fastest as well.' That was the opinion of *Motor* magazine when the cars were new in 1967.

These Rovers filled the gap as ministerial transport in Britain when the Humbers ceased production in 1967 and continued to sell quite strongly, even though their design was now quite elderly. By this stage, they had very little competition. Jaguars were not only more expensive, but lacked the dignity and patrician air that these Rovers embodied so fully. Vanden Plas and Wolseley had now followed Humber and Alvis into the history books (in fact, Rover had bought Alvis in 1965), and there were no home-grown alternatives at the price. The Rover P5B remained available into 1973, and in their last few years was a glorious but much-loved anachronism.

This 1972 Rover, one of the last of its kind, was still in use as ministerial transport in early 1981, when it was pictured outside Number Ten, Downing Street.

The New
JAGUAR 4·2 LITRE MARK TEN

WITH NEW ADVANCED DESIGN XK ENGINE · NEW POWER STEERING
NEW AUTOMATIC TRANSMISSION OR NEW ALL SYNCHROMESH GEARBOX
and many other important new features

This new, more powerful model retains all the luxury of spacious seating for five, fine leather upholstery, centre folding armrests, reclining front seats, folding picnic trays, deep pile carpets, all-round independent suspension, self-adjusting disc brakes on all four wheels and large capacity boot—and incorporates many new features including NEW 4.2 litre 6 cyl. twin overhead camshaft advanced design of race-proved Jaguar engine, five times winner of Le Mans, which gives increased acceleration and flexibility, NEW Borg Warner Model 8 Automatic Transmission or NEW four speed all-synchromesh Gear Box, NEW Marles 'Varamatic' Bendix Power Steering (exclusive to Jaguar), NEW effortless braking with separate fluid system for front and rear, NEW cooling system, NEW Selective Car Temperature Control, Alternator for higher charge at lower engine r.p.m. and pre-engaged starter. All these new features bring increased performance, safety and comfort to "a special kind of motoring which no other car in the world can offer."

PRICES FROM £2156.0.5. (inc. P.T.)

LONDON SHOWROOMS: 88 PICCADILLY W.I.

THE SPORTING DIMENSION: ALVIS, LAGONDA AND JAGUAR

NOT EVERYBODY WHO wanted a top-quality car wanted a grand saloon that would look right with a chauffeur at the wheel. The archetype of the alternative in the interwar years had been the Bentley – a gentleman's carriage, for sure, but one with high performance and a distinguished sporting heritage. Although times had changed by the start of the 1950s, there was still a demand for this type of car, and three companies in particular catered for it.

They were Alvis, Jaguar and Lagonda. In the 1920s and 1930s, Alvis had built some of Britain's most sophisticated and exclusive fast cars, to become a serious rival for Bentley. Lagonda had even employed W.O. Bentley as a designer during the 1930s, after Rolls-Royce had bought his old company, and had built some truly formidable and glamorous sporting machinery.

Jaguar, meanwhile, had a rather different image, resulting from traditional British upper-class social attitudes. Jaguar lacked the pedigree of Bentley, Alvis or Lagonda, having only been founded (as SS Cars) in 1935. So it was seen as a pretender to the status of these established marques. That did not stop the company selling its luxury saloons by the thousand (it had a profitable sports car range as well), while Alvis and Lagonda struggled with annual production figures in the hundreds. It was clear which way the wind was blowing.

Lagonda was the oldest of these three companies, and by the mid-1920s was building high-quality sporting saloons,

Opposite: The 1961 Jaguar Mk X was a large, sleek saloon that perhaps pandered too much to the taste of the US market; even its creator, Sir William Lyons, felt it had grown too big. This advertisement is for the 4.2-litre model that was introduced in 1964.

Although its engineering was advanced for the time, the 2.6-litre Lagonda, which took the company into the 1950s, was quite conservative in appearance.

but an over-complex range led it into financial difficulties. It survived through refinancing to build some superb luxury chassis in the later 1930s, with a high-performance bias. Cash flow remained a problem, however, and the new car designed by W.O. Bentley for the post-war market had to wait until 1948 and a company takeover by tractor-maker David Brown before there was enough money to build it. Brown bought Aston Martin too, and in later years there would be a close relationship between the two marques.

The Lagonda saloon of the early 1950s embodied some advanced engineering for the time, thanks to W.O. Bentley and his team. Its all-round independent suspension was not common in those days. At this stage, the twin-overhead-camshaft engine had only a 2.6-litre capacity, but with a high 105-bhp output that allowed a 90-mph top speed. From 1952, Mk II versions had 125 bhp and correspondingly more performance. Visually, however, the car's style dated quickly.

From 1953, Lagonda raised the engine capacity to 3 litres and the power to 140 bhp, adding a more modern and streamlined body constructed by the coachbuilder Tickford, which would soon become part of the David Brown stable.

The first examples had only two doors, but a four-door saloon arrived in 1954 and quickly became the primary product. Sadly, sales of this excellent car proved disappointing, no doubt because of its cost: at nearly £3,700, inclusive of purchase taxes, in 1956, this gentleman's sporting carriage was selling for sub-Bentley money when there were cheaper cars with better performance. A drastic price cut for 1957 brought the cost below £3,000, but it was too late. The Lagonda disappeared that year and was not replaced.

A determined attempt to revive the marque in 1961 with the Lagonda Rapide was a

failure. Touring of Milan created a sharply styled four-door saloon body in the favoured Italian idiom of the time, and the car was built on a long-wheelbase version of the Aston Martin DB4 chassis, with a sophisticated new rear suspension and the Aston's hugely powerful six-cylinder engine. Despite the automatic gearbox expected in a luxury saloon by this time, 130 mph was still possible on unrestricted roads. Unfortunately, the oddly styled nose and the huge launch price of over £5,000, inclusive of purchase tax, were handicaps. The buyers could not be found, and the Rapide ceased production in 1964 after just fifty-four had been made. For many more years, that would be the last the world would hear of Lagonda.

Alvis, meanwhile, tried a different tack. After a reasonably successful attempt to revive a 1930s design immediately after the war, it developed a new chassis and engine for 1950

In 1953, Lagonda came out with a 3-litre engine and a new, more modern body style. The two-door sports saloon pictured here was supplemented by a four-door saloon with similar lines from 1954.

Alvis modernised the appearance of their 1940s saloon body for the TC21 or 3-litre model. This is an early example of the 100-mph TC21/100 model.

that would carry on in its essentials right through until the marque's demise in 1967. Alongside saloons that looked like the older models, there were some grand drophead coupés and even a few rather odd roadsters, but the definitive early 1950s Alvis cars did not arrive until 1953, when the TC21 and TC21/100 were introduced.

The same old four-door saloon body was used, but the engine now delivered 100 bhp and a top speed that bordered on 100 mph. The TC21/100 had more power again, and came with the guarantee of 100 mph that gave the car its new name. Air scoops in the bonnet and wire wheels suggested its more sporting performance. Though old-fashioned enough in concept to be a true gentleman's sporting carriage, its performance brought Alvis properly into the 1950s.

Sadly, the TC21/100 – often called the Grey Lady after the 1953 motor show car painted that colour – could not last. Its bodies came from the coachbuilder Mulliners of Birmingham, who sold out to car maker Standard-Triumph in 1955. Alvis promptly acquired the rights to a body designed by the Swiss coachbuilder Graber and created the first of a long and successful line of two-door sports saloons. But, if these continued in the great tradition of the gentleman's sporting carriage, they were not luxury saloons. No dowager duchess would be seen clambering into or out of the back past the tipped-forward passenger seat. Rover bought Alvis in 1965, and the replacement model it conceived – though unfortunately never built – was a two-door coupé. Alvis had changed forever.

Jaguar had got going again after the war with some nicely styled sports saloons based on prewar models and using engines originally designed by Standard. These same engines also powered the transitional Mk V model, built between 1949 and 1951 with a brand-new chassis under its warmed-over prewar bodywork. This was a fine sports saloon of its day with a 90-mph top speed, and had an attractive traditional British wood and leather interior. Unfortunately, Jaguar had not yet reached its peak, and indifferent build quality encouraged the perception that the Jaguar was trying to pass itself off as a poor man's Bentley.

Jaguar was a pioneer of rear spats on British saloon models, as seen here on a 1950 3.5-litre Mk V saloon. These cars still used Standard-derived engines.

JAGUAR
wins
Monte Carlo Rally
outright

(Subject to official confirmation)

to add to these outstanding International successes

INTERNATIONAL RACES

LE MANS *(Three Times)*
T.T. *(Twice)*
RHEIMS *(Twice)*
SEBRING *(Twice)*

INTERNATIONAL RALLIES

ALPINE *(9 Coupes des Alpes – 1 Coupe d'or)*
R.A.C. Great Britain *(Twice)*
LIEGE-ROME-LIEGE
TULIP

Congratulations to Mr. Ronald Adams and his crew on their outstanding performance with their privately entered standard production Mark VII Saloon.

LONDON SHOWROOMS : 88 PICCADILLY, W.1

Spats and sweeping wing lines also characterised the Mk VII Jaguars that followed, although these cars had Jaguar's own twin-overhead camshaft XK engine. This advertisement dates from 1956, and makes clear that the car was a sporting success as well as a sales triumph.

Meanwhile, Jaguar had developed its own new engine, and the glorious 3.4-litre XK type of 1948 with its twin overhead camshafts would go on to make the marque's reputation over the next two decades. At first available only in the XK120 sports car, this became available from 1950 in the new Jaguar saloon. The car was called the Mk VII (Bentley had already laid claim to the Mk VI name that would have been logical), and it was a simply stupendous machine. It was capable of the magic 100 mph and yet had all the space and interior appointments of much more expensive sports saloons from the traditional manufacturers, and a modern-looking four-door body to boot. Uprated to Mk VIIM standard in 1954 with the latest 190-bhp version of the engine, the car became a favourite with motor sport enthusiasts too.

Mk VIIM gave way in 1956 to Mk VIII, which added a one-piece windscreen, two-tone colour schemes, and the latest 210-bhp version of the XK engine. This was really too much for its all-drum braking system, so when the Mk IX arrived in 1958 as the last model in this line of big sports saloons, it had disc brakes all round. The engine was more powerful again, now boasting 220 bhp from 3.8 litres. Power-assisted steering was standard, and the car could manage all of 114 mph.

These later versions of the big Jaguar did not sell as well as the Mk VII and Mk VIIM, which had achieved an annual average of more than 7800. Their figures of a little over 3000 a year were nevertheless not depressed by any inadequacies, but by the availability of comparable performance in the

new 'compact' Jaguars that arrived in 1955 at much lower prices. But it is important to see these figures in context. In the 1950s, no other luxury car maker in Britain apart from Humber could even approach sales quantities like these. Jaguar was obviously getting something right.

Many Jaguar sales were made in the USA, and for its next big saloon the company embraced American dimensions; it was a risk worth taking when the compact saloons were selling strongly at home. So the Mk X of 1962 was a larger saloon with a more streamlined and modern shape. Powered

Mk VII was followed by Mk VIIM, Mk VIII and Mk IX, all based on the same elegant and imposing shape. This is a late Mk IX model.

The Jaguar's dashboard design was beginning to look dated by the time of the Mk IX in 1959, but the swathes of figured wood and big steering wheel were in the great British luxury saloon tradition.

New JAGUAR 3·4 & 3·8 'S' *models*

join the famous range of Mark 2, Mark Ten,   & 'E' type models which continue unchanged

The latest development of one of the world's most successful cars

The new 'S' models make available in a car of compact dimensions, the very latest refinements in Jaguar design and engineering.

The wide choice of high-performance high-quality motoring which the Jaguar range already provides, is now further extended by the introduction of these new 3.4 and 3.8 'S' models. With impeccable body styling and spacious interior proportions, these cars are powered by the world famous Jaguar XK engine of either 3.4 litre or 3.8 litre capacity. The many important features incorporated include:—

- All round independent suspension providing the utmost riding comfort under all conditions.
- Self adjusting Disc Brakes on all four wheels and self adjusting handbrake.
- Driver operated variable interior heating with on or off control for rear compartment.
- Reclining seats for driver and front passenger.

- An exceptionally large luggage boot giving an entirely unobstructed cubic capacity of no less than 19 cubic feet.
- Twin petrol tanks—one in each rear wing with change-over switch in dash panel.
- Spacious interior with generous head and leg room affording the highest degree of comfort.

See the Jaguar range including the   new 'S' models on Stand 118 Earls Court

---

Adding features of the Mk X saloon to the smaller Mk 2 saloons produced the S-type Jaguars in 1963, available with either 3.4-litre or 3.8-litre engines.

by the 265-bhp 3.8-litre engine used in the new E-type sports model, it also incorporated Jaguar's latest independent rear suspension. Power-assisted steering and an automatic gearbox were only to be expected (although a few cars had manual gearboxes with overdrive), and the vast interior had Jaguar's usual combination of figured wood veneer, leather upholstery and aircraft-like instrumentation.

From 1964, the engine was uprated to 4.2 litres but with the same 265 bhp, and a limousine derivative, with all the changes inside the passenger cabin, arrived a year later. It remained rare. In 1966, Mk X became 420G as new names were adopted across the range, gaining a side trim-strip and a few interior changes. It remained available until 1970, by which time the new and sleeker XJ6 model had already been introduced as its replacement.

This last of the big Jaguars sold nearly as well as the Mk VIIIs and Mk IXs, but it was too big and unwieldy

The S-type was further upgraded with the 4.2-litre engine as a 420. This was the dashboard – a superb blend of the traditional and the modern.

to satisfy those buyers who wanted a sporty Jaguar luxury saloon. So some of its engineering improvements, and much of its styling, were applied to the compact models to create the S-type in 1963 and the 420 in 1966. These picked up the missing Jaguar customers, and a Daimler-badged version of the 420 called the Sovereign helped ensure a wider spread of sales. It was Jaguar and Daimler that survived into the 1970s: by that time, both Lagonda and Alvis were long gone.

Although legroom was at a premium in the smaller Jaguars, wood and leather created the appropriate interior ambience.

You can judge a car by the company it keeps.

They'd called you in at the last moment. 'You'll be a steward, of course' they'd said.

You'd done it last year and you were looking forward to a little relaxation.

But still, you knew them all and they were a good bunch. It wouldn't stop you enjoying yourself.

So you piled the family into the 3-Litre, stuck the sticker on the windscreen and now here you are.

The 3-Litre does you well. In your life you need a big car.

Not some cheap mutton dressed as expensive lamb.

Nor something so expensive you have to wait months for it. But a car you can trust in the country.

Like any good thoroughbred the 3-Litre is made to be driven. Made to carry five in space and comfort.

Moving on independent self-levelling Hydrolastic® suspension it takes smoothly, quietly, impressively to your kind of life.

Your kind of driving.

The 3-Litre is a real saloon, meticulously built in the best tradition of Austin engineering.

For people like you who want to drive an expensive car. Not just to own one.

Recommended price from £1,592 (inc. p.t.).

With automatic transmission £104 extra (inc. p.t.).

Extra is charged for delivery, radio, wing mirrors, spot lights, seat belts and number plates.

AUSTIN

Austin 3-litre, built like a thoroughbred.

THE GREAT PRETENDERS: BMC

THE GAP BETWEEN the big family saloon and the luxury saloon was bridged by a variety of models from the British Motor Corporation. BMC had been formed in 1952 by a merger of the two big players in the volume-production field, Austin and Nuffield. The Nuffield Group had been built around the Morris marque, but by this time included MG, Riley and Wolseley; Austin's contribution was itself, the Vanden Plas coachbuilding company it had bought in 1946, and the powerful personality of its chairman, Len Lord. It was not long before Lord became the dominant figure in BMC too.

Of the marques united under BMC, only Austin and Wolseley had any track record in the luxury saloon business. Austin had always had a big saloon for the carriage trade during the interwar years. Wolseley had been the quality brand within the Nuffield empire since 1927, although its focus had been on owner-drivers and its cars had been better-equipped derivatives of more mundane Morris models.

Austin introduced a new large chassis in 1946, offering it in two guises. The A110 Sheerline had fashionable razor-edged styling that gave it a passing resemblance to the new Bentley Mk VI, while the A120 Princess had a more sophisticated and expensive-looking body that was coach-built by Vanden Plas in London. They were underpowered, and both quickly took on an enlarged 4-litre engine, being renamed A125 and A135, the figures reflecting the brake horsepower of their new

Opposite: The idea of the 'right company' emerged again in this 1969 advertisement for the Austin 3-litre, but this appeal to snobbery did not help to sell the cars.

Austin's A135 Princess was a grand limousine, and later carried Vanden Plas badges. Note the chauffeur waiting in the background on this publicity picture for the car.

engine; that in the Princess was again the more powerful. Top speed was about 75 mph, but these cars were built for those who wanted grandeur, not speed.

The Sheerline was really a little crude in its engineering, and its blocky wooden dashboard looked dated even when new. Yet it hit a waiting market, and Austin sold 9000 before 1954, averaging 1125 examples a year. Of these, one in ten had a limousine body. The Princess, which was nearly twice as expensive, continued to sell right through until 1968. That such an old design should have lingered on so long was purely because it had all the presence of a Rolls-Royce or Daimler while being much cheaper.

Austin's A110 was the cheapest version of BMC's 3-litre range, and is seen here as a late model registered in 1967. The 'tail fins' were a late-1950s imitation of American styling fashions.

A six-window limousine joined the ranks in 1952, and options such as an automatic gearbox, power-assisted steering and servo-assisted brakes refined the car over the years. From 1957, it was renamed as a Princess 4-litre, and the Austin name discreetly disappeared; no doubt it was seen as too everyday for the pretensions of this big limousine. Then, from 1960, it was renamed again, as the Vanden Plas Limousine. Nevertheless, only 5257 of all types were built in fourteen years – an average of about 375 a year. In the British Leyland corporate scheme, they were replaced by the Jaguar-based Daimler DS420 limousine.

There was one more model in this complex line-up of luxury cars from BMC, and that was the Princess IV. Strictly an Austin, although never badged as such, it had a new and more modern-looking body by Vanden Plas on a reworked version of the old chassis, and a new 4-litre engine with 150 bhp. It is hard to understand why this attractive car was a miserable failure, but just 200 were built before BMC dropped it in 1959.

Gradually rationalising the models from the various marques it had inherited, BMC embarked in the later 1950s on a process that has always been derisively known as 'badge-engineering'. That meant designing a single model but dressing it with different marque badges, levels of equipment and other cosmetic features to provide a series of different

If the A110 was only masquerading as a luxury saloon, it certainly made a good job of doing so. This sales brochure picture shows the well-appointed interior, with wood and leather in the appropriate quantities.

A different grille and two-tone paintwork characterised the more expensive Wolseley version of the big BMC saloons. This one is a 1959 Wolseley 6/99.

The Wolseley's dashboard was deliberately more upmarket than the Austin's, with heavily figured wood veneer.

models. In its large-car ranges, badge-engineering arrived in 1959 with the first two of an eventual three-car range. These were the Austin A99 Westminster and the Wolseley 6/99. The name of the Austin, with its suggestion of senior officialdom and parliamentary office, revealed the model's aspirations.

They were in effect the same car. Both had a 103-bhp six-cylinder engine of 2.9 litres, a three-speed column-change gearbox with standard overdrive, disc front brakes and the option of an automatic gearbox. Both used the same body with fashionable fin-shaped rear wing tops, a design created for BMC by the Italian styling house of Pinin Farina. The Wolseley had two-tone paint, a traditional upright grille and auxiliary lamps recessed into the front panel. It was also better trimmed than the Austin. It was more expensive too: in 1959, the Austin cost £1,148 12s 6d, including purchase tax, while the Wolseley's price was £1,254 17s 6d.

Top of the BMC 3-litre range was the Vanden Plas 3-litre, seen here as a 1960 model. The body shape was almost unchanged, but the grille and other cosmetic details distinguished this car from the Austin and Wolseley models. The almost formal look of the paintwork helped create the right impression.

Both these cars were priced just a little below the mainstream luxury saloon market, but the third model of the trio would be pitched right into the most keenly contested sector. This was the Vanden Plas 3-litre, introduced in 1960 with a slightly modified version of the same body that had gained a Vanden Plas-style radiator grille. Its engine was the same 2.9-litre six-cylinder, despite the name. Much more important was that the car was trimmed and finished at the Vanden Plas works to the coachbuilder's traditional standards, and the wood and leather interior was really a very nice place

This was the dashboard of the Vanden Plas 3-litre, deliberately more traditional in appearance than that of the Austin or Wolseley. It was arguably less attractive – but perhaps that did not matter if only the chauffeur was going to use it.

to sit. A selection of sober, sophisticated colour schemes helped it look the part of the refined and sophisticated luxury saloon. All this justified its higher launch price of £1,396 10s 10d, including purchase tax, which still made it cheap in comparison with most of its competitors.

None of these early models could reach 100 mph. So, in 1961, the engines were uprated to give 120 bhp; a four-speed gearbox replaced the three-speed-plus-overdrive type; and modified rear suspension improved the handling. Those who bought the Austins and Wolseleys (now known as A110 and 6/110 types respectively) certainly appreciated the changes. Both cars became popular with police forces across Britain for traffic duties.

The Austin A110 and Wolseley 6/110 soldiered on until 1968, but the Vanden Plas marque struck out on its own from 1964, when the 3-litre gave way to a model called the 4-litre R. This was much more expensive: the first models had a showroom price of £1,995 6s 3d, including purchase tax, and had the task of replacing a model that had cost £1,346 12s 11d. That strategy turned out to be a major miscalculation for BMC.

The Vanden Plas 4-litre R was a further variation on the big BMC saloons, this time with a 4-litre Rolls-Royce engine, a bigger price tag and plenty of snob appeal. It did not sell well.

The 4-litre R was the product of an alliance between Rolls-Royce and BMC. Rolls-Royce had wanted to introduce a new lower-cost Bentley model, and the plan was to use the big BMC saloon body with a six-cylinder Rolls-Royce engine of 4 litres. Other refinements traditional to the marque would have been added, but the Bentley Java project was cancelled in 1962. Undaunted, BMC picked it up and ran with it, modifying the body slightly, getting Vanden Plas to do the luxury trimming, buying in the Rolls-Royce engine and fitting an automatic gearbox as standard.

The problem was that the Vanden Plas 4-litre R offered little that set it apart from the old 3-litre car. Though smooth and powerful, the Rolls-Royce engine was nowhere near as powerful as its claimed 175 bhp suggested, and the 4-litre R was just a few miles an hour faster than the 3-litre. Buyers were unimpressed to discover that they were paying a huge premium for the privilege of the Rolls-Royce name and not much else. BMC struggled to sell the car: in four years only 6999 were sold, and in 1968 British Leyland management decided to halt its production. That average of 1750 cars a year compared poorly with the 2540 average for the old 3-litre model, and there were better cars from other marques in the British Leyland stable.

One result of all this was that the big Vanden Plas cars were not directly replaced, although the name survived on luxury-trim versions of the little BMC 1100 and 1300 models, and on the Daimler DS420 limousine. Nor was the Wolseley directly replaced. Once production of the A110 Westminster and the 6/110 came to an end in 1968, their replacement was badged solely as an Austin.

In fact, the new Austin 3-litre had been announced a year earlier, in 1967. It was a typical piece of BMC corporate thinking, uniting the centre section of the spacious 1800 'Land Crab' saloons with a larger boot, and replacing their transverse engines and front-wheel drive by a conventional

This was the interior that welcomed rear passengers in the Vanden Plas 4-litre R. It had the expected mixture of leather and wood with picnic tables – but more differences from the cheaper models might have helped sell more cars.

Perhaps Vanden Plas 4-litre R customers expected something better for their money than this rather cheap-looking plastic badge on the car's wings.

north-south engine and rear-wheel drive. Thinking that the new model needed to fit somewhere near the top end of the market segment that the old Austin and Wolseley 3-litre models had occupied, BMC introduced it at a price of £1,470 11s 0d, or £1,516 13s 4d with automatic gearbox.

Unfortunately, this was far too expensive for what it offered. The undeniable truth was that it was not pretty, it offered no more passenger space than the very much cheaper Austin 1800, and the Austin badge was too downmarket for a car of these pretensions. Even the performance was lacklustre; it could only just manage 100 mph – about 3 mph less than the models it replaced. Perhaps leather upholstery would have helped too.

One way or another, production of the Austin 3-litre ended in 1971, after just under 10,000 had been built. The average of 2500 a year over four years was nowhere near the 4580 a year that the old A99/A110 Austins had achieved and, if the Wolseley and Vanden Plas variants of those are taken into account as well, the average production for the Pinin Farina-designed cars totalled over 10,900 a year. After this ignominious failure, British Leyland wisely chose to leave the big luxury saloon sector to their Rover marque.

FURTHER READING

British luxury cars of the 1950s and 1960s have, by and large, not been well covered in books. However, for anyone who is interested in finding out more about the cars that figure in this volume, here is some recommended reading:

Clarke, R.M. *Armstrong Siddeley Gold Portfolio (1945–1960)*. Brooklands Books, 1991.
Clarke, R.M. *Rolls-Royce Silver Cloud & Bentley S Series: Ultimate Portfolio*. Brooklands Books, 2003.
Sedgwick, Michael, and Gillies, Mark. *A–Z of Cars: 1945–1970*. Bay View Books, 1989.
Taylor, James. *Rover P5 and P5B: The Complete Story*. Crowood Press, 1997 and 2007.
Thorley, Nigel. *Jaguar Mark VII to 420G: The Complete Companion*. Bay View Books, 1994.

PLACES TO VISIT

British Motor Museum, Banbury Road, Gaydon, Warwickshire CV35 0BJ. Telephone: 01926 641188.
Cotswold Motoring Museum & Toy Collection, The Old Mill, Bourton-on-the-Water, Gloucestershire GL54 2BY. Telephone: 01451 821255.
Coventry Transport Museum, Millennium Place, Hales Street, Coventry CV1 1JD. Telephone: 024 7623 4270.
Haynes International Motor Museum, Sparkford, Yeovil, Somerset BA22 7LH. Telephone: 01963 440804.
Lakeland Motor Museum, Old Blue Mill, Backbarrow, Ulverston, Cumbria LA12 8TA. Telephone: 01539 530400.
National Motor Museum, Beaulieu, New Forest, Hampshire SO42 7ZN. Telephone: 01590 612345.

INDEX